DESERT CLIMATES

Cath Senker

capstone

Edited by Linda Staniford
Designed by Philippa Jenkins
Original illustrations © Capstone Global Library Limited 2017
Illustrated by Oxford Designers and Illustrators
Picture research by Svetlana Zhurkin
Production by Victoria Fitzgerald
Originated by Capstone Global Library Ltd

20 19 18 17 16
10 9 8 7 6 5 4 3 2 1

Library of Congress Cataloging-in-Publication Data
Library of Congress Cataloging-in-Publication Data is available on the Library of Congress website.
ISBN: 978-1-4846-3781-4 (library hardcover)
ISBN: 978-1-4846-3785-2 (paperback)
ISBN: 978-1-4846-3797-5 (eBook PDF)

This book has been officially leveled using the F&P Text Level Gradient™ Levelling System.

Acknowledgments
We would like to thank the following for permission to reproduce photographs: Alamy: Arterra Picture Library, 36, Graphic Science, 23; Courtesy NaDEET, 30, 31; Dreamstime: Piotr Zajda, 34, Pulpitis, 26; Getty Images: AFP/Fadel Senna, 35, Gamma-Rapho/Jean-Luc Manaud, 27, John Cancalosi, 17, UIG/Auscape, 22; Newscom: Barry Iverson Photography/Barry Iverson, 32, Eye Ubiquitous, 9, Photoshot/Wolfgang Kaehler, 15, robertharding/Olivier Goujon, 7, Sipa USA/Pacific Press, 39; NPS: Kurt Moses, 40; Shutterstock: Anton Foltin, 10, 41, Arcangelo, 13, asharkyu, 11, Bandurka, 18, Chris Curtis, 45, Christian Musat, 16, eFesenko, 29, 43, Federico Massa, 44, gkuna, 4, Gordan, back cover and throughout, jiawangkun, 28, Jose Ignacio Soto, 24, Juancat, 33, Ksenia Ragozina, 8, Laborant, 19, Marina Khlybova, cover, orin, 21, PammySue, 12, Petr Salinger, 14, Photo travel VlaD, 37, Steve Bower, 20, Tim Roberts Photography, 42, Valeriya Repina, 25; Wikimedia, 38

We would like to thank Dr Sandra Mather, Professor Emerita, Department of Geology and Astronomy, West Chester University, West Chester, Pennsylvania, USA, for her invaluable help in the preparation of this book.

Every effort has been made to contact copyright holders of material reproduced in this book. Any omissions will be rectified in subsequent printings if notice is given to the publisher.

All the Internet addresses (URLs) given in this book were valid at the time of going to press. However, due to the dynamic nature of the Internet, some addresses may have changed, or sites may have changed or ceased to exist since publication. While the author and publisher regret any inconvenience this may cause readers, no responsibility for any such changes can be accepted by either the author or the publisher.

TABLE OF CONTENTS

WHERE ARE THE DESERT CLIMATES?....................................4

WHAT IS A DESERT CLIMATE? 6

WHICH PLANTS LIVE IN THE DESERT REGIONS? 10

    FEATURE: ROSE AND RHUBARB – EXTRAORDINARY
PLANTS OF THE MIDDLE EAST 14

WHICH ANIMALS LIVE IN DESERTS?............................ 16

    FEATURE: CAMELS – CREATURES OF THE DESERT 18

    FEATURE: AUSTRALIA'S DESERT ANTS 22

WHO LIVES IN DESERT CLIMATES?............................... 24

    FEATURE: NAMIBIA – SUSTAINABLE DESERT LIVING......................30

WHICH RESOURCES ARE FOUND IN DESERTS?..............................32

    FEATURE: DEVELOPING SOLAR POWER IN THE DESERT 34

WHAT ARE THE THREATS TO DESERT CLIMATES? 36

    FEATURE: "CITIZEN SCIENTISTS" RECORD CLIMATE CHANGE 40

HOW CAN WE PROTECT DESERTS?..42

GLOSSARY...46

READ MORE.. 47

INDEX 48

Some words are shown in bold, **like this**. You can find out what they mean by looking in the glossary.

WHERE ARE THE DESERT CLIMATES?

When most people think of a desert, they probably think of a wide expanse of sand in boiling-hot sunshine. Many deserts are indeed hot. But some are cold places. A desert is a large area of extremely dry land. Any place with less than 10 inches (25 centimeters) of precipitation (rain or snow) a year is classified as a desert.

The Negev is a rocky desert in Israel.

BAKING-HOT DESERTS

Most hot deserts are at low **latitudes** around the Equator up to about 30° north and south, near the Tropic of Cancer and the Tropic of Capricorn. They include the Sahara in northern Africa, the Kalahari in southwestern Africa, and the Victoria of Australia. Deserts cover a large area of Saudi Arabia and stretch to Iran, Pakistan, and western India. In Baja California and the interior of Mexico in North America, there are deserts too, while South America has the Atacama Desert.

Amazing fact

Deserts cover about one-fifth of Earth's land and are found on every continent.

This map shows the desert regions of the world.

ARCTIC OCEAN

Arctic Circle

NORTH AMERICA

EUROPE

ATLANTIC OCEAN

ASIA

Tropic of Cancer

AFRICA

Equator

PACIFIC OCEAN

SOUTH AMERICA

INDIAN OCEAN

Tropic of Capricorn

AUSTRALIA

Key

Desert regions

ANTARCTIC OCEAN

Antarctic Circle

ANTARCTICA

COLD DESERTS

Cold deserts form at higher latitudes — in central Asia, western North America, southeastern South America, and southern Australia. They include the Patagonian Desert in South America, the Taklamakan in China, and the Gobi in Asia. Believe it or not, frozen Antarctica is a desert!

DESERT LIFE

Deserts might seem lifeless at first, but there are plants, animals, and even people living in these regions. Various kinds of **drought**-loving plants make their home in the dry conditions. Hiding from the Sun are animals specially **adapted** to the harsh environment. Some **indigenous** peoples have a traditional way of life, while others have settled in desert cities.

WHAT IS A DESERT CLIMATE?

Desert climates vary. Deserts can be cold at night, cold deserts are sometimes warm, and some have more rain than others.

SWELTERING HEAT

Hot deserts are the driest and hottest places on Earth. During the afternoon, temperatures can reach a scorching 122 degrees Fahrenheit (50 degrees Celsius) or higher. That is seriously hot! Deserts are hot because of the lack of water. The Sun shines on the ground and heats it. The heat rises into the air.

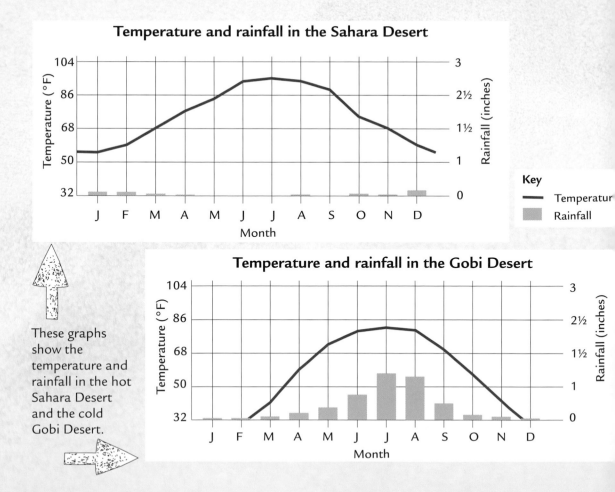

These graphs show the temperature and rainfall in the hot Sahara Desert and the cold Gobi Desert.

Amazing fact

The record for the highest temperature in the world is held by Greenland Ranch in Death Valley, California. It hit a scorching 134°F (56.7°C) on July 10, 1913.

RARE RAIN

Hot deserts have hardly any rain. Why is there so little? As air at the Equator rises and cools, the water vapor in the air condenses, turning into water drops. The water drops form clouds and fall as rain over the tropical regions. The air moves north and south to about 30° latitude on either side of the **tropics** and sinks. As it sinks it becomes warmer and drier, so any remaining moisture **evaporates.**

 DID YOU KNOW?

At night, even hot deserts can be cold. With little vegetation and no clouds in the sky, much of the daytime heat quickly escapes into space after sunset. The temperature drops dramatically.

SUDDEN DOWNPOURS

Desert rainfall is extremely unpredictable. Some years, it doesn't rain at all. When it does rain, sometimes all the year's rain arrives in just a few days or even on one day.

One of the driest places on Earth is the Atacama Desert in Chile, South America. In the northern town of Arica, Chile, an average of less than 0.02 inch (0.05 cm) of rain falls each year. But in October 2015, a downpour of 0.9 inch (2.3 cm) of rain fell in one day. Flower seeds that had been buried in the ground for years began to grow. The desert bloomed with brightly colored blossoms. This only happens about every five to ten years.

The flowers in the Atacama Desert in Chile last for only a very brief time.

DID YOU KNOW?

The largest hot desert is the Sahara, in Africa. The largest cold (non-polar) desert is the Gobi, in Asia. "Sahara" and "Gobi" both mean "desert" in the local languages — so they are both called "desert desert" in English!

MORE RAIN

In contrast to the Atacama and most other deserts, the Sonoran Desert in North America has more rainfall. It is still dry and hot, but it has a lot more vegetation and wildlife than other desert regions.

A PLACE OF EXTREMES

For extremes of hot and cold, check out the Gobi Desert. In this cold desert, winter temperatures plunge to an average low of −40°F (−40°C). That's way too cold to step outdoors for very long. Winters are long and cold, and the temperature remains below freezing for much of the year. Yet the summer is unbearably hot and dry, with temperatures hitting 113°F (45°C) in July.

Snow covers the Gobi Desert in the Mongolian winter.

WHICH PLANTS LIVE IN THE DESERT REGIONS?

In hot deserts, there are no trees to be seen and very little vegetation — just some short grasses and desert shrubs. Then there's a downpour. Soon, the desert blooms. In the Mojave Desert, in the southwestern United States, bright sunflowers appear.

Houseplants will die if left without water for a week or so. But desert plants can survive for years without fresh water. They simply become dormant (inactive), waiting for the rains. Some have long root systems so they can reach water deep underground. Others have shallow roots that spread out to absorb dew on the surface of the soil. Their leaves have a small surface area, so they don't lose much water through evaporation.

Many colorful flowers grow in the Mojave Desert, including desert marigolds and desert asters.

The agave is a succulent originally from Mexico. "Succulent" means "juicy."

QUICK WORK

When it rains and temporary lakes flood the dry land, the plants revive as if by magic. Seeds that had lain dormant for many years, waiting for the right conditions, now sprout. They quickly develop leaves and flowers, seeds ripen in a matter of days, and then the plant becomes dormant once again.

There are other ways for plants to survive too. Some desert plants, called **succulents,** store huge amounts of water in their cells. The waxy surface of their leaves stops water from escaping.

DID YOU KNOW?

A fan cools you down because moving air increases evaporation. For plants, that means losing precious water. Desert marigolds have hairs, which slow the air moving over the plant and help keep in the moisture.

CACTI TACTICS

In the North American and South American deserts, cacti thrive. Their roots spread out widely under the surface of the ground. When it rains, they absorb water from a broad area and store it in their thick, fleshy stems. A tough, waxy coating stops moisture from escaping. The cacti's sharp spines scare off thirsty animals.

Cacti are strange plants. They either have tiny leaves or none at all. How can a plant survive without leaves? The stem does the job of carrying out photosynthesis — making food from sunlight, water, minerals, and carbon dioxide in the air.

The Mexican Desert in Arizona and California is home to the saguaro cactus. With large white flowers and bright-red edible fruit, it can grow to an impressive 50 feet (15 meters) tall. That's about three times the height of a giraffe!

The prickly pear is a cactus we can eat. The spiky skin must be peeled carefully to eat the delicious fruit.

COLD DESERT VEGETATION

To survive in cold deserts, plants have to cope with extreme heat and cold as well as little water. Like hot desert plants, they often have long roots to find water and few leaves. Many are deciduous. In the summer, the leaves make food. The leaves fall off in the winter to save energy.

In the Gobi Desert, the saxaul tree collects water under the bark, which thirsty travelers can squeeze for a drink. Its roots grow up to 30 feet (9 m) deep. Wild onions grow in dry, rocky areas. The leaves of wild onions are dense and packed together to prevent them from drying out. The onions are small, and people say they taste like hazelnuts.

 DID YOU KNOW?

Plants don't move, do they? But what's that giant ball tumbling around in the North American desert? It's tumbleweed. It can be as small as a soccer ball or as big as a car, and it does tumble around, scattering its seeds as it rolls along.

13

ROSE AND RHUBARB – EXTRAORDINARY PLANTS OF THE MIDDLE EAST

What's that tight ball of dead-looking dry leaves on the ground in the Judaean Desert, in Israel? The leaves and seedpods are curled inward. The ball is not even rooted to the ground. A gust of wind blows it around like tumbleweed. Surely it can't still be alive after years of dry weather?

RESURRECTION

The Rose of Jericho can indeed spring back to life. Just a few hours after a downpour, the leaves uncurl to form a green plant 12 inches (30 cm) wide, with tiny white flowers. It's been nicknamed the Resurrection Plant, after the resurrection of Jesus Christ. Resurrection means coming back to life.

After rain, the Rose of Jericho transforms itself from the dead-looking ball of leaves on the left to the live green plant on the right.

Amazing fact

Desert rhubarb collects as much water as Mediterranean plants, which benefit from more than five times as much rainfall in one year.

Desert rhubarb grows in the dry, rocky Gobi Desert. Looking a bit like garden rhubarb, it has a long, single root underground rather than a set of shallow roots like most desert plants.

SELF-WATERING

Perhaps even stranger is the desert rhubarb plant, which can water itself! Researchers showed that this plant, in the mountains of the Negev Desert in Israel, absorbed 16 times more water than other plants nearby.

The Negev Desert has an average of just 3 inches (75 millimeters) of rainfall a year — around the same as the state of Georgia receives in one spring month. The desert rhubarb needs to keep every drop it can get. It has between one and four massive leaves, up to 28 inches (70 cm) wide, in a rosette shape. Looking a bit like cabbage leaves, the leaves have deep grooves in them and are covered with wax. Rain that falls on the leaves goes down the grooves, glides over the wax coating, flows into the middle of the rosette, and travels directly down to the root below.

WHICH ANIMALS LIVE IN DESERTS?

Desert animals can't usually be seen in the heat of the day. They mostly take shelter out of the Sun and only emerge at night to feed. Many get their moisture from their food, so they don't need fresh drinking water.

LIVING IN THE HOT DESERT

Food is hard to find in deserts. There is little vegetation for plant-eating animals to feed on. Meat-eating animals often eat the remains of dead animals. Reptiles such as snakes and lizards are better at surviving in the desert than mammals and birds, because they don't need as much food.

Dining on scorpions

Some animals have adapted so that they can eat food that other animals cannot eat. The sand goanna of the Australian desert can feast on scorpions. The scorpions sting them with poison that would make a person howl in agony, but it doesn't harm the tough little goanna.

The fennec fox is the smallest fox in the world, but its ears look like they belong to a much larger animal.

Amazing fact

More than half of desert animals stay underground in holes or burrows during hot weather. It's cooler underground and there is more moisture.

Big ears, cool body

Mammals that make their homes in the desert have special features. The tiny fennec fox of the Sahara Desert has enormous ears — but they're not there for super-sensitive hearing. Fennecs lose body heat through their ears, which keeps them cool. They have long, thick hair to protect them from the Sun in daytime and also keep them cozy at night. They're not fussy about their diet, eating plants, rodents, reptiles, and even insects. They get most of the water they need from the food they eat, so they rarely need to drink water.

Some desert mice build shelters from fallen cactus spines to protect themselves from predators such as coyotes and hawks.

DID YOU KNOW?

Some species of deer and antelope such as the Dorcas gazelle and Addax antelope of the Sahara pass almost all of their waste as pellets. They lose little precious water by urinating.

Store pouches

Kangaroo rats and pocket mice are found in the Sonoran Desert. During the day, they rest in their underground burrows. At night, they search for seeds, storing them in their cheek pouches like hamsters. These little rodents never need to drink water. They get all the water they need from the seeds they eat.

CAMELS — CREATURES OF THE DESERT

Camels are adapted to live in parched desert conditions. They can travel across the Arabian Desert without water for a week in summer and two weeks in winter. How do they do it?

The secret lies in the camel's large hump — or two humps if it's a Bactrian camel. This odd body part is formed of fat and muscle. When it's tall and firm, the camel is well fed. After several days without food, the hump goes limp and leans to one side.

Bactrian camels in the Gobi Desert have a thick, warm coat in winter, which they shed as the temperature rises.

Amazing fact

Our body temperature can only vary by 2°F (1°C) but a camel's body temperature can vary by up to 13°F (6°C).

NO SWEAT

Camels store water in fat cells, and they're good at making it last. When people get hot, they have to perspire (sweat) to lower their body temperature. Camels don't sweat. When they get hot, their body temperature rises, and they don't lose water through perspiration. At night, their bodies cool down. By morning, their body temperature has fallen and they feel cool again, ready to face the hot day ahead.

SAND STOPPERS

In the desert, the sand gets everywhere. Camels have adapted to cope with sand. They have pads on their knees, leg joints, and chest to protect them when kneeling down. Long eyelashes protect their eyes from sand storms and the Sun. Their nostrils can open wide for breathing or close to keep out the sand.

A camel's thick eyebrows shield its eyes from the Sun, and it has hair inside its ears to keep out the sand.

LIVING IN THE COLD DESERT

To survive extreme cold in winter and sweltering heat in summer, hardy cold-desert creatures have some unique adaptations.

Jackrabbits

Black-tailed jackrabbits live in the southwestern deserts of the United States. They have huge, thin ears to help them control their body heat. When it's hot, the blood flow through the ears increases, so heat escapes and the jackrabbit cools down. In cold weather, the blood flow decreases, so the ears keep in the heat.

The black-tailed jackrabbit is adapted to eat desert species such as cacti and sagebrush.

DID YOU KNOW?

The greater roadrunner of the southwestern deserts in the United States is a tough little bird. It eats insects, scorpions, lizards, and other desert animals, and can even prey on rattlesnakes. Strangely, it prefers running to flying. If it needs to flee from danger, it can run faster than a person — up to about 20 miles per hour (32 kilometers per hour).

Desert tortoises are able to remember where they have dug their water basins so that they do not get too thirsty.

Gazelles, gerbils, and tortoises

In the Turkestan desert of central Asia, gazelles, gerbils, and tortoises roam. Gazelles eat desert shrubs and leaves. They feed in the early morning or evening, when the plants have the most moisture content. Gerbils use their sharp claws to build underground tunnels in the sand. They stay in these tunnels during the day, as it is cooler underground. The tunnels also keep them safe from predators. The gerbils emerge in the early morning to gather food.

The desert tortoise might look clumsy, plodding along on its short, stumpy legs. But its claws are designed to allow it to walk easily on the sand. The tortoise uses them to dig its own mini water pools that trap rainwater, so that it can enjoy a long, refreshing drink. Desert tortoises store water inside their bodies too — they can reuse water from their bladder before it is lost. They escape the extreme winter and summer temperatures in their underground burrows.

AUSTRALIA'S DESERT ANTS

Australia is home to more than 1,000 species of ants. Many of these species have developed ways to cope with the harsh desert conditions.

BULLDOG ANTS

Bulldog ants got their name for a good reason. They are 1.6 inches (4 cm) long and very aggressive: they can easily rip the wings off a wasp. Yet they cooperate among themselves.

The hunters search for food and bring back insects and reptiles to feed the **colony.** The builders dig chambers over 6 feet (up to 2 m) underground for shelter from the Sun and predators. Tucked away in the safest area is the queen, looked after by other ants. The queen produces larvae, which will become the next generation of ants. Working together is the best way of surviving in the extreme climate.

Female bulldog ants look after larvae in the nest chamber.

Amazing fact

A meat-ant nest can contain more than 64,000 ants.

This honeybee is soon overpowered by a group of vicious meat ants.

MEAT ANTS

Australia's meat ants are team workers too. Young ants care for ants and larvae, while older ants forage for food. Every morning they fan out to hunt for grasshoppers and other insects that have died in the night. When the older ants find an insect, they tear it up with their strong jaws and carry the parts back to the nest. In hot weather they rest in the cool nest until the Sun goes down.

There are more meat ants on the desert ground than any other creature. In addition to feeding their colony, they are nature's helpers. Building large nests helps to introduce air into the soil, which is healthy. The ants remove dead materials from around their nest and bring their rotting prey underground, which helps to make the desert soil **fertile.**

Since ancient times, people have lived by **oases, wadis,** and rivers. They provide water to the people. The water also makes the soil fertile and the land fruitful.

At the oasis near Tinerhir, Morocco, farmers have dug channels to irrigate their crops.

OASIS BOUNTY

Oases can be huge, covering many acres. They form when water comes up to the surface of land from springs and wells underground. Farmers grow many crops on the land around oases. At North African and Asian oases, date palms tower above the other plants, creating shade below. Date palms have long roots that can reach the underground water, so they don't need to be **irrigated.** Beneath the date palms, apricot, olive, orange, and pomegranate trees flourish. Farmers also plant crops such as millet, barley, wheat, rice, cotton, and sugarcane. In the past, it was hard work to pull up water from underground and irrigate crops by hand. Now, farmers often have motorized pumps.

Wadis are dry streambeds that fill with water during rare rain showers. Some follow the route of underground streams. Plants have long roots to reach the underground water.

This sugarcane plantation is on the bank of the Nile River, in Egypt. Today, irrigating the crops is expensive, and small farmers earn little because the price paid for sugarcane is low.

FERTILE FLOODPLAINS

Rivers cross all large deserts. The Nile in Egypt, the Tigris and Euphrates in Iraq, the Indus in Pakistan, and the Colorado in the United States are all rivers that cross deserts. When rivers flood, they leave behind **nutrients,** making the soil of the floodplains good for farming. In Egypt, farmers live alongside the fertile Nile. For more than 5,000 years, they have dug canals to bring water from the river to distant fields so they can cultivate a broader area.

DID YOU KNOW?

The Rum Farm in Wadi Rum, Jordan, grows food for the whole country. Fruits such as apricots, nectarines, grapes, and figs and vegetables including egglplants, squash, and potatoes are grown there. The farm is located above a large aquifer, a layer of porous rock that can hold water. Succulents are planted to support the crops. They reduce evaporation of water from the soil and lower the surface temperature of the soil.

INDIGENOUS PEOPLES OF THE DESERT

Deserts might look empty, but there are people who make their homes in this harsh environment. Groups of indigenous farmers and herders have a traditional way of life that is suited to desert conditions.

Bedouin nomads

For thousands of years, the deserts of the Middle East and Africa have been home to Bedouin **nomads.** Across the region, the Bedouin move around frequently so that they don't use up all of the resources in one area. They breed camels, Arabian horses, and sheep. Some groups of Bedouin stay in an area long enough to cultivate dates and other crops.

A Bedouin man lives the traditional way of life in the Sahara Desert in Morocco.

Amazing fact

The Sahara Desert is nearly as big as the United States, but only has about 2.5 million people — less than 1 person per square mile (0.4 per square km). The U.S. population is more than 321 million!

Some Bedouin still live the traditional way of life today. The Chaamba Bedouin can be found in the central Algerian Sahara. Their black tents are made in the traditional way using goat hair. For protection from the fierce Sun, the people wear light, loose-fitting clothes from head to toe. Only their faces, hands, and feet peek out. They make most of their food from the milk of camels and goats.

But times have changed for most Bedouin. Many are settled and no longer move from place to place with their herds. They travel in four-wheel drive vehicles and their children go to school.

 DID YOU KNOW?

The Tubu are desert dwellers in Niger. The men tend the herds of cattle, while the women travel with their camels to trade cheese, dried meat, and camels for cereals and other foods. The Tubu women are remarkably skilled at finding wells in the vast expanse of the desert. With no map, the women **navigate** by counting the ridges of sand dunes. They use the Sun to guide them and check the shadows made by the dunes to decide which direction to go. At night, they navigate using the North Star.

DESERT LIFE IN LAS VEGAS

In Las Vegas, Nevada, in the Mojave Desert, the contrast with traditional desert lives could not be greater. No tents here! People have comfortable homes, electric power for lighting and air-conditioning, and travel everywhere by car. There are large-scale water and **sewerage** systems, and yards with luxurious green grass. But it isn't green because of rain. The Mojave Desert only has 2 to 6 inches (5 to 15 cm) of rain each year. Ninety percent of Las Vegas's water is taken from Lake Mead, a huge **reservoir** about 30 miles (48 km) away on the Colorado River, and the rest comes from groundwater.

In May 2016, the water level in Lake Mead sunk to the lowest ever, due to heavy use and climate change.

Amazing fact

In Las Vegas, 219 gallons (829 liters) of water are used per person per day. But the authorities are making great efforts to reduce this. Residents are not allowed to water their lawns between 11 a.m. and 7 p.m., when the Sun is at its hottest and much of the water simply evaporates. The city pays people cash if they get rid of their lawns!

EGYPT'S NEW CITIES

Cities in developing countries such as Egypt are a massive drain on resources too. Since the 1970s the government has been building new cities in the desert, such as El-Sadat and El-Obour. The new cities were intended to encourage people to leave their old overcrowded communities. But there aren't enough jobs. People are forced to drive to the old cities to work each day, creating heavy traffic and misery for commuters. Empty spaces in the new cities are planted with lawns or golf courses, which have to be watered. A great deal of energy is used to treat and pump water so it is safe to drink. Desert cities like these are not **sustainable.** But it doesn't have to be like this.

In normal daily traffic in Cairo, Egypt, many rely on cars, and public transportation is poor.

NAMIBIA — SUSTAINABLE DESERT LIVING

The Namib Desert Environmental Education Trust Center (NaDEET) trains local people of all ages to adopt a sustainable lifestyle in the desert. What happens here?

THE 3 RS

Schoolchildren practice the 3 Rs: reduce, reuse, recycle. They're shown how to use solar ovens and cookers, so they don't need to buy wood or spend hours collecting firewood, which destroys valuable trees. The solar ovens and cookers use the heat from the Sun, so the children cook with them between 10 a.m. and 3 p.m., when the Sun is at its hottest. They put their meals in hot boxes to keep them warm.

NaDEET runs on electricity from solar power — sunshine is plentiful in the desert. Solar power also heats the water for washing and showers.

The children at NaDEET cook their own lunches on the solar cooker.

A boy at NaDEET washes his hands from a bottle of water rather than a running faucet.

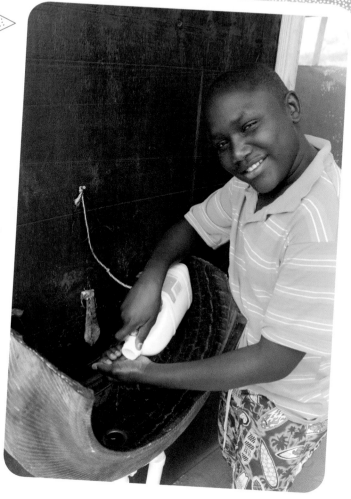

WATER WISE

After a day of activities, the children have a bucket shower, using a simple bucket with a small hole in the bottom and a shower attachment. It uses just 3 gallons (12 liters) of water, compared to 6 gallons (23 liters) for a three-minute regular shower with a water-saving showerhead. The children brush their teeth with cups of water rather than using a faucet, and there are long-drop **compost** toilets. Instead of flushing with water, the waste drops into a deep pit. These simple methods save time and money, and help the environment too.

DID YOU KNOW?

At NaDEET, trash is sorted into paper, glass, cans, food waste, and other waste. The paper is used to make fire bricks, the food waste is composted, and the glass and cans are recycled. Little is left to be burned or to go to landfill.

WHICH RESOURCES ARE FOUND IN DESERTS?

A wealth of resources lies beneath desert rock and sand. In the 20th century, explorers discovered oil. This "black gold" has been pumped out and **exported** all around the world to power factories, machines, and vehicles. The economies of Middle Eastern countries depend on the sale of oil.

This oil and gas exploration plant is in Saudi Arabia, where there are known to be vast fuel reserves.

In the Thar Desert, in India, workers mine limestone and gypsum (used in making plaster) for the building industry. In the North American and South American deserts, copper and other metals are found. Salt pans — wide, flat areas, covered with salt — are located in the Atacama Desert in Chile. Water evaporates to leave salt shining white on the ground. Companies collect the salt and sell this "white gold."

Amazing fact

More than half of the known oil reserves are under the Arabian Desert, in countries including Saudi Arabia, Iraq, and Iran. Saudi Arabia has more oil reserves than any other country.

DESERT TRAVEL

Beautiful landscapes are a resource too. Tourists looking for a challenge head to deserts for grueling rock climbing, hiking, or dirt biking, and tourism brings in money.

Backpackers explore the desert in Utah.

DID YOU KNOW?

Desert trips without a local guide are risky. Three women got lost on a trip to Death Valley, California, in 2010. They slept in their car overnight and rolled up the windows to avoid curious mountain lions. The following day, they signaled to airplanes with a yellow emergency blanket, but no one spotted them. By day three, they were dangerously short of water. Amazingly, they discovered some old trailers containing food and water, giving them hope they would survive. That evening, a deafening noise came from the sky — a rescue helicopter! Their ordeal was over.

DEVELOPING SOLAR POWER IN THE DESERT

Deserts are a major source of oil, but using this **fossil fuel** is contributing to **global warming.** Luckily, in the desert there is also a key resource to help solve this problem. The sunny climate is perfect for developing large-scale solar power.

IVANPAH

Ivanpah solar complex in California, in the Mojave Desert, is one of the largest solar thermal (heating) power plants in the world. How does it work?

• More than 300,000 mirrors track the Sun and focus its rays on boilers on top of tall towers.
• Sunlight strikes the pipes in the boilers and heats the water to make steam.
• The steam travels in pipes to a turbine, which produces electricity.

The three plants at Ivanpah generate enough electricity for more than 140,000 homes in California.

This is Ivanpah solar plant in California. The state aims to source one-third of its energy from renewable sources by 2020.

Amazing fact

Morocco is one of the sunniest countries in the world. It receives about 3,000 hours of sunshine per year, an average of more than 8 hours a day.

The huge array of solar mirrors at Noor-Ouarzazate in Morocco covers 1,112 acres (450 hectares).

NOOR-OUARZAZATE

Morocco's solar power plant Noor-Ouarzazate, on the edge of the Sahara Desert, is even bigger than Ivanpah. It can generate up to 160 megawatts of power, enough for 650,000 people. And this is just phase one of the development. By 2018 it will produce up to 580 megawatts of power — as much as a small nuclear reactor — and provide electricity for more than one million people. Like Ivanpah, the solar farm uses curved mirrors — 500,000 of them. The plant can even generate power at night and store the heat in a tank of molten salts. The Moroccan government hopes that its desert climate will allow it to produce 52 percent of its power from **renewable** sources by 2030. One day, it could even export energy north to Europe and east to Saudi Arabia.

WHAT ARE THE THREATS TO DESERT CLIMATES?

There's no question about it: deserts are spreading because of overuse of the land — it's called desertification. This is not a good thing, as previously fertile land becomes dry and less useful. At the same time, the existing desert habitats are also under threat from industry, tourism, and climate change.

Cows graze in the Sahel in Mali. Desertification of areas like the Sahel occurs because of overuse of resources: grazing too many animals, farming too much land, and collecting too much firewood.

BATTLE OF THE SPECIES

Nomads move on before they exhaust the resources. But many people have settled in areas near deserts, such as the Sahel, where they're putting pressure on the land. Their livestock munch the desert plants. Farmers introduce non-native plants to feed their grazing animals. But the new plants compete with native species, and desert animals lose their natural habitat.

SALTY SOIL AND TREE LOSS

Farmers have to water their crops, but it can cause salinization — too much salt in the soil. As water evaporates, it draws salts from the soil to the surface. The salts are poisonous to many plants, making it harder to grow crops.

People also harvest trees for fuel. When trees are removed, the soil is left bare. The wind can blow it away. This is called soil **erosion.** The quality of the soil becomes poor and isn't good for supporting crops.

HARMING HABITATS

Oil and gas production and mining can also damage desert habitats. They can disturb habitats, pollute the soil or air, or cause harm through oil spills. Vehicle tires can press the soil down, making it difficult for plants to regrow.

Deserts are wild and beautiful places, and tourists love to explore them. But their off-road vehicles can damage plants and disturb the soil, leaving it open to wind erosion.

DID YOU KNOW?

Scientists are looking into salt-loving plants that could become popular foods in the future — samphire is already eaten in salads. But people won't be able to eat these plants in large amounts because they're too salty.

Tourists in Dubai enjoy off-road adventures, driving on desert sand dunes in 4x4 vehicles, but this can cause pollution and damage the environment.

Amazing fact

Tracks of vehicles used in World War II (1939–1945) are still visible in the desert sands of North Africa, after more than 75 years.

CLIMATE CHANGE

Deserts are already hot and dry. How could global warming affect them?

Desert die-offs

A small change in temperature or rainfall could have dramatic results on a desert. The Great Victoria Desert, in Australia, is likely to suffer from more days with super-high temperatures and a decrease in the already low rainfall. As climate changes, it will be a case of the "survival of the fittest"; unlucky plants and animals might become extinct. Already, in the Sonoran Desert in North America, some birds do not breed during severe droughts. Cold deserts are growing hotter too, and species that cannot move to cooler areas might die out.

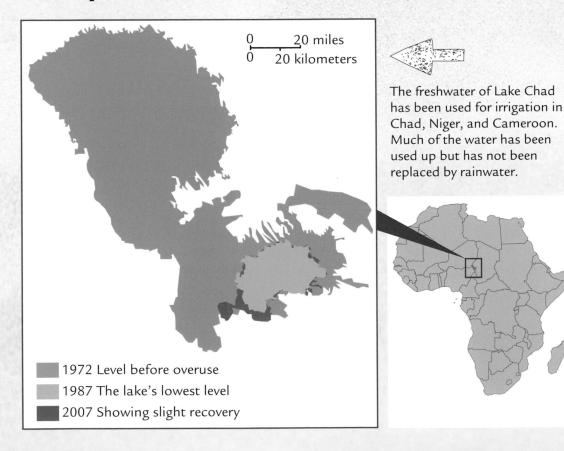

0   20 miles
0   20 kilometers

The freshwater of Lake Chad has been used for irrigation in Chad, Niger, and Cameroon. Much of the water has been used up but has not been replaced by rainwater.

1972 Level before overuse
1987 The lake's lowest level
2007 Showing slight recovery

These migrants from sub-Saharan Africa are on their way to Italy, hoping for a better life.

Drought and wildfire

Global warming contributes to desertification, turning more dry areas into deserts. It is likely there will be more droughts, water holes might disappear, and plants and animals may no longer be able to survive. As temperatures rise and droughts grow longer, there could be more wildfires, destroying the few remaining trees and shrubs and speeding up desertification further.

Forced to flee

In the Sahel region in Africa, global warming is shrinking Lake Chad, the soils are losing fertility, and land is turning to desert. People in this already poor area depend on farming for their livelihoods. There are few other jobs available. Some people have abandoned their lands and moved to North Africa, hoping to find work. Global warming is adding to the already huge migration crisis. People who have lost everything travel from country to country, seeking another way to survive.

"CITIZEN SCIENTISTS" RECORD CLIMATE CHANGE

In the desert of Joshua Tree National Park in California, Earthwatch volunteers walk around with notebooks and GPS navigation devices. Led by scientists from the University of California, the volunteers are "citizen scientists." They monitor and record the wildlife so they can measure the changes over time. It's part of a long-term project to find out how climate change is affecting the desert. Joshua Tree National Park stretches from the low-lying, hot Sonoran Desert to the higher and cooler Mojave Desert. The varying temperatures make it ideal for this research.

 A "citizen scientist" collects data with Earthwatch volunteers in Joshua Tree National Park.

Amazing fact

Using computer modeling, scientists have predicted that over the next 100 years, Joshua trees will disappear from their national park habitat.

WILDLIFE COUNT

To survey an area, the scientists divide it into plots. The volunteers record the numbers of plants and iguanas, desert tortoises, wrens, quails, and other creatures that they spot in each plot. They set pitfall traps — hiding plastic buckets in holes in the ground so that small animals such as scorpions and pocket mice fall in. The scientists count the animals and let them go.

WINNERS AND LOSERS

The team has already noticed major changes as the average temperature has risen. The Joshua trees are dying out. Some other trees and shrubs cannot cope with the rising temperatures in the Sonoran Desert but are doing well in higher, cooler areas. But who knows how many will succeed in moving to a cooler habitat? It's the same for birds and animals. Scientists have found tortoises that have died during severe droughts. Some animals find it easier to move or adapt than others. Those that can't will be the losers to climate change.

Joshua trees need a cold period of weather to flower, so as the temperatures rise, the trees are dying out.

HOW CAN WE PROTECT DESERTS?

Climate change is here, and in the short term we can't stop it. But there are ways to resist desertification.

CROPS, PLANTS, AND WATER

Instead of growing single crops, farmers could return to rotating crops — switching the crops they grow in each plot every year to keep the soil fertile. Also, leaving some areas fallow (without crops) for a while can allow the soil to rest and become fertile again. It's useful to plant crops from the pea family such as acacia. The pea plants take nitrogen from the air and put it in the ground, restoring the soil's fertility. Bushes and trees can be planted to replace those that have been cut down. They will help to keep the soil in place.

Farming uses about 70 percent of Arizona's water, and water resources are being used more quickly than they can be replaced. People need to find ways to manage the land better and use less water for irrigation.

This traditional Islamic-style courtyard with a garden in Uzbekistan naturally protects people from the desert heat.

IN TUNE WITH NATURE

People in desert cities can reduce their water use. Grass lawns have no place in dry climates. Instead, gardeners can raise drought-loving plants that are native to the region, such as saltbushes and emu bushes from Australia. These plants have beautiful pink or yellow flowers and won't need much watering, so they save time too. People can reuse water. "Gray" water from washing dishes and showers is fine for watering the garden.

DID YOU KNOW?

Old Middle Eastern cities are designed to protect people from the heat in simple ways. In Shibam, South Yemen, the streets are narrow and the buildings tall, shading the streets below. Only people on foot or bikes use these streets. People shop in covered outdoor markets. Homes are built around courtyards with pools and leafy plants to keep them cool and shaded.

WORST CASE, BEST CASE

In the worst-case scenario, we continue relying on oil, gas, and coal, causing climate change and damage to the environment. Desertification turns one-third of Earth's land masses into desert. These areas suffer from long droughts, native plants and animals become extinct, and people can no longer survive there. In desert cities, people use water heavily and growing numbers of cars increase pollution.

In areas that have turned to desert, animals might die out and people might be forced to abandon the land.

DID YOU KNOW?

Communities could become more sustainable by adopting some of the features of early cities, before the days of cars and air-conditioning. Porches or awnings added to buildings provide shade so people can sit outside comfortably, while planting trees along sidewalks makes walking in the heat more pleasant. Improving bus and train services can reduce car use and the pollution it causes, making cities quieter and healthier places.

CHANGE FOR THE BETTER

Communities in desert regions adopt sustainable technologies. They build solar power plants, using the near-constant sunshine, and conserve water wherever possible. In rural communities, everyone has compost toilets and bucket showers. Farmers and herders cooperate to preserve desert habitats, and native plants and animals flourish once more.

GLOSSARY

adapt change in order to survive; a change in an animal or plant is called an adaptation

colony community of animals or plants of one kind living close together

compost rotted animal or vegetable waste that helps to make the soil fertile and good for growing crops

drought period when there is a lack of rain, leading to a shortage of water

erosion wearing away of rock or soil by wind, water, ice, or sand

evaporate change from a liquid to a gas by adding heat to the liquid — for example, water turning into water vapor in the air

export sell to other countries

fertile good for the growth of crops

fossil fuel fuel such as coal or oil, which was formed over millions of years from the remains of animals or plants

global warming slow increase in the overall temperature of Earth's atmosphere

indigenous one of the original peoples of a land

irrigate to water crops because there is not enough rain for them to grow well

latitude distance of a place north or south of the Equator

navigate find your way using maps or using the Sun and features in the landscape

nomad someone who moves from place to place in search of grazing land for animals

nutrient substance that is vital for a plant or animal to live and grow

oasis fertile spot in a desert where water is found; the plural of "oasis" is "oases"

renewable source of energy that does not run out, such as solar power

reservoir lake where water is stored

sewerage system of drains to take away waste from homes and buildings

succulent plant with thick, fleshy leaves or stems adapted to storing water

sustainable way of doing things that does not destroy natural resources

tropics area between the Tropic of Cancer, north of the Equator, and the Tropic of Capricorn, south of the Equator

wadi bed or valley of a stream in regions of southwestern Asia and northern Africa that is usually dry, except during the rainy season

READ MORE

BOOKS

Clarke, Ginjer L. *The Gobi Desert.* What's Up In . . . New York: Grosset & Dunlap, 2016.

Desert. Let's Explore. Oakland, Calif.: Lonely Planet, 2017.

Hardyman, Robyn. *Surviving the Desert.* Sole Survivor. New York: Gareth Stevens Publishing, 2016.

Spilsbury, Richard, and Louise Spilsbury. *At Home in the Desert.* New York: PowerKids Press, 2016.

FACTHOUND

Use Facthound to find Internet sites related to this book.
Just type in 9781484637814 and go!

PLACE TO VISIT

Arizona-Sonora Desert Museum, Tucson, Arizona

www.desertmuseum.org
Find out all about the Sonoran Desert.

INDEX

animals, 16–23
Antarctica, 5
ants, 23
Arabian Desert, 33
Atacama Desert, Chile, 8, 32
Australia, 22–23

Bedouin nomads, 26
    way of life, 27
bulldog ants, 22

cacti, 12
camels, 18–19
climate change, 42, 44
    research, 40–41
cold deserts, 5, 9
    animals, 20–27
    temperature, 9
crops, 24
    rotating, 42

date palms, 24
Death Valley, California, 33
desertification, 36–37, 38, 42, 44
desert mice, 17
desert rhubarb, 15

Egypt, new desert cities, 29

fennec fox, 17

gazelles, 21
gerbils, 21
global warming, 38–39
Gobi Desert, Asia, 8, 9
Great Victoria Desert, Australia, 38

hot deserts, 4, 8
    temperature, 6–7

jackrabbits, 20
Joshua Tree National Park, California, 40–41

kangaroo rats, 17

Lake Chad, Africa, 38–39
Las Vegas, Nevada, 28

meat ants, 23
mining, 32, 37
Mojave Desert, California, 10, 28, 34

Namib Desert Environmental Education Trust Center (NaDEET), 30–31
Negev Desert, Israel, 15

oases, 24
oil, 32, 33, 34, 37

people, 24–29, 36, 39
plant adaptations, 10–15
prickly pear, 13

rainfall, 7, 8, 9
rivers, 25
roadrunners, 20
Rose of Jericho (Resurrection Plant), 14

Sahara Desert, 8, 35
salt pans, 32
samphirel, 36
sand goanna, 16
saxaul tree, 13

soil erosion, 37
solar power, 30, 34–35, 45
solar power plants
    Ivanpah, California, 34
    Noor-Ouarzazate, Morocco, 35
Sonoran Desert, United States, 9, 38
succulents, 11, 25

Thar Desert, India, 32
tortoises, 21
tourism, 33, 37
Tubu people, 27
tumbleweed, 13

wadis, 24
water use, 43, 45
    Las Vegas, 28
wildfires, 39
wild onions, 13